SAINS

Quick and Easy
Food for Toddlers

HEALTHY RECIPES FOR UNDER-FIVES

Jacqueline Bellefontaine

Contents

Published exclusively for J Sainsbury plc
Stamford House Stamford Street
London SE1 9LL

by Martin Books
Simon & Schuster Consumer Group
Grafton House 64 Maids Causeway
Cambridge CB5 8DD

Published 1995

ISBN 0 85941 887 1

© 1995 Martin Books

Printed and bound in the UK by Bath Press Colourbooks
Design: Green Moore Lowenhoff
Photography: Steve Baxter
Styling: Marian Price
Food preparation: Jane Stevenson
Typesetting: Goodfellow & Egan Ltd, Cambridge

Pictured on the front cover: Easy Mini Pizza Faces (page 64)

Introduction

Every parent wants to give their child a good start in life, and there are few things more important than a healthy diet. By establishing a good and balanced diet for your toddler you will be laying the foundations for lifelong healthy eating habits, as well as ensuring that your child is getting all of the nutrients that he or she needs to grow healthy, fit and strong.

This book has been written with both nutrition and convenience in mind, and the recipes are designed to fit in with a busy family's life. You will find them quick and easy, requiring little effort or time. You can begin to use the recipes once your child is a year old and is consuming a variety of foods. There is no need to wait until he or she can eat 'proper meals'; once your child is eating the various foods in a given recipe, simply remove a portion of the dish and purée it, remembering to do this before seasoning.

Your health visitor will be able to give you information on when to introduce different foods such as fruit, vegetables, cereals, meat and dairy products to your toddler's diet. There are many books available on the subject, and most baby magazines regularly have features on weaning. If you are at all worried about any aspect of your child's diet, always seek advice from your health visitor or doctor.

Although as a nation we consume too much fat and refined carbohydrates and too few fruits and vegetables, it is important to remember that a low-fat, high-fibre diet is not suitable for toddlers. Toddlers have relatively high energy and nutrient requirements, and a high-fibre diet will fill them up without supplying them with the necessary energy and nutrients. Fats are needed to supply essential fatty acids and fat-soluble vitamins (although too much saturated animal fat should be avoided). Milk and dairy products should also be an integral part of any toddler's diet.

The recipes for cakes and bakes in this book have been designed to supply a balance of nutrients using limited fat and sugar. Sugar is perhaps the number one enemy in a toddler's diet because although it supplies energy it is a major cause of tooth decay. Try to encourage a taste for savoury rather than sweet foods.

A healthy diet is a balanced diet supplying all of the nutrients required for life. These nutrients are supplied in 5 main food groups:

1 Meat, poultry, eggs and fish – for protein.
2 Milk and dairy products – for calcium, fat-soluble vitamins and protein.
3 Cereals and pulses – for carbohydrates and fibre.
4 Fruits and vegetables – for vitamins, minerals and fibre.
5 Oils, fatty and sugary foods.

If you give your child a variety of foods from the first 4 food groups and sparingly from the fifth, they are likely to be eating a balanced diet.

STRESS-FREE FEEDING FOR TODDLERS

• Encourage your child from the start to eat a wide variety of different foods – he or she is less likely to become a fussy eater later on.
• Try not to be too anxious if your child refuses to eat certain foods – meal times should be fun, not a battlefield.
• Youngsters naturally like sweet tastes and adding fruit to savoury dishes may encourage them to eat certain foods.
• Toddlers who won't drink milk may enjoy milk puddings or accept other dairy foods such as cheese or yogurt, which will supply the calcium and protein they need.
• Make foods appear fun – try arranging vegetables to form mini-faces; use biscuit cutters to shape sandwiches or scones into animals, stars or hearts; serve drinks with coloured straws.
• Finger foods are often popular and give your child independence at meal times from a very early stage. Several of the dishes in this book are just right for eating using fingers.
• If you have time, involve your child in the preparation of meals. This is a good way to encourage an interest in food.
• Large portions of food can be overwhelming for a young child: offer smaller portions and let them come back for more.

HOW MUCH FOOD IS ENOUGH?

It is hard to give serving sizes for toddlers. Appetites vary enormously from child to child, and from day to day. Let your own child be your guide. Offer them plenty of fruit or other healthy snacks and treats between meals. And don't worry – if your toddler is full of energy and has a zest for life, he or she is almost certainly eating enough.

RECIPE NOTES

All recipes in this book give ingredients in both metric (g, ml, etc.) and Imperial (oz, pints, etc.) measures. Use either set of quantities, but not a mixture of both, in any one recipe.

All teaspoons and tablespoons are level, unless otherwise stated. 1 teaspoon = a 5 ml spoon; 1 tablespoon = a 15 ml spoon.

Egg size is medium (size 3), unless otherwise stated.

Vegetables and fruit are medium-size unless otherwise stated.

Freshly ground black pepper should be used throughout.

PREPARATION AND COOKING TIMES

Preparation and cooking times are included at the head of the recipes as a general guide; preparation times, especially, are approximate and timings are usually rounded to the nearest 5 minutes.

Preparation times include the time taken to prepare ingredients in the list, but not to make any 'basic' recipe.

The cooking times given at the heads of the recipes denote cooking periods when the dish can be left largely unattended, e.g. baking, and not the total amount of cooking for the recipe. Always read and follow the timings given for the steps of the recipe in the method.

Breakfasts

Most experts agree that breakfast is the most important meal of the day. It restores blood glucose levels after a night of fasting and provides the energy needed to set one up for the day. Of course, breakfast is important for adults too – so if you frequently skip it, now is the time to get back into the breakfast habit.

Yogurt, fruit or a piece of toast is ideal if time is very short. Cereals fortified with vitamins and minerals are also suitable, but do not serve those with added fibre as these may fill your toddler up without supplying enough energy and nutrients.

Toddler Muesli

Preparation time: 15 minutes.
Freezing: not recommended. Makes 550 g/1 lb 2 oz (approximately 18 servings).

Adult muesli is not suitable for babies and toddlers as it often contains quite large pieces of nuts, which may present a choking hazard. Wheatgerm has been added to this recipe as it provides a valuable source of thiamin (vitamin B1) and iron. You can double the quantities if you like, as this recipe can be stored for 2–3 months in a sealed container.

25 g (1 oz) ready-to-eat dried apricots
25 g (1 oz) ready-to-eat prunes
250 g (8 oz) porridge oats
50 g (2 oz) wheatgerm

50 g (2 oz) sultanas
50 g (2 oz) raisins
50 g (2 oz) ground almonds or hazelnuts
2 tablespoons dried milk powder

❶ Place the apricots and prunes in a food processor and process until roughly chopped.

❷ Add the oats, wheatgerm, sultanas and raisins and process again as required. For older toddlers, process until just combined. For younger toddlers, process slightly longer.

❸ Stir in the ground nuts and milk powder. Store in an airtight container for up to 12 weeks.

❹ To serve, spoon into a bowl and add milk, fruit juice or yogurt. Stir and allow to stand for a few minutes before serving.

French Toast Fingers

Preparation and cooking time: 10 minutes.
Freezing: not recommended. Serves 2.

French toast is a delicious finger food and the perfect breakfast for those who have trouble in making their little ones sit still for 5 minutes in the morning. For a special treat serve with a little maple syrup.

125 ml (4 fl oz) full-cream milk
1 egg
a pinch of ground nutmeg

2 slices bread
a small knob of butter or margarine

❶ Beat together the milk, egg and nutmeg until well combined.
❷ Soak the bread in the beaten egg mixture until well coated.
❸ Heat the butter or margarine in a heavy-based frying pan and cook the bread until it's lightly golden. Carefully turn it over and cook the second side until just golden.
❹ Allow to cool slightly and cut the bread into fingers to serve.

Sultana and Cinnamon Drop Pancakes

Preparation and cooking time: 25 minutes.
Freezing: recommended. Makes 10.

Children will love these tasty, easy-to-eat pancakes.

125 g (4 oz) self-raising flour
¼ teaspoon ground cinnamon
15 g (½ oz) butter or margarine
50 g (2 oz) caster sugar

75 g (3 oz) sultanas
1 egg, beaten lightly
4 tablespoons full-cream milk
oil for cooking

❶ Sift the flour and cinnamon into a large bowl and rub in the butter with your fingertips.
❷ Stir in the sugar and sultanas.
❸ Make a well in the centre of the mixture. Pour the beaten egg and milk into the well and beat with a wooden spoon, gradually incorporating the dry ingredients.
❹ Heat a heavy-based frying pan over a medium heat and add just enough oil to coat the base lightly.
❺ Drop rounded spoonfuls of the mixture into the hot frying pan and spread slightly with the back of the spoon.
❻ Cook for 2–3 minutes each side, or until just golden. Cook 3–4 pancakes at a time, repeating until all the mixture has been used. Add a little oil to the pan between batches if necessary. Serve the pancakes warm on their own, or topped with a little natural yogurt.

Porridge with Apricots and Raisins

Preparation and cooking time: 10 minutes.
Freezing: not recommended.
Serves 1 adult + 1 child.

You can make this in the microwave if you like. Although it won't save much time, it does eliminate the risk of the porridge catching and burning on the bottom.

50 g (2 oz) porridge oats
25 g (1 oz) ready-to-eat dried apricots, chopped
25 g (1 oz) raisins
150 ml (¼ pint) full-cream milk

150 ml (¼ pint) water
a pinch of ground cinnamon
To serve:
honey
milk

❶ Place the oats, apricots, raisins, milk, water and cinnamon in a small saucepan and bring gently to a simmer, stirring occasionally.
❷ Simmer gently for 2–3 minutes, stirring constantly to prevent the porridge from sticking to the base of the pan. Add a little extra water if the mixture becomes too thick.
❸ Sweeten with honey to taste, and serve with a little milk poured over the porridge.

Savoury Egg Scramble

Preparation and cooking time: 15 minutes.
Freezing: not recommended. Serves 1–2 children.

Make sure the egg is completely cooked before serving. This nourishing breakfast can be made more fun by cutting out shapes from toast to serve with it.

25 g (1 oz) frozen diced mixed vegetables
1 egg
1 tablespoon full-cream milk

a knob of butter or margarine
1 tablespoon cottage cheese with chives
toast, to serve

❶ Cook the vegetables according to the pack instructions, drain and keep warm.
❷ Beat the egg and milk together.
❸ Melt the butter or margarine in a small saucepan and add the egg mixture. Cook gently over a low heat, stirring until the mixture scrambles and the egg is just cooked.
❹ Stir in the cottage cheese and cooked vegetables and toss over the heat until warmed through.
❺ Serve with lightly buttered toast, cut in shapes with cookie cutters if desired.

Packed Lunches and Light Meals

It is often the case that you need a meal for just your toddler or for yourself and your toddler, and as a busy parent, you don't have too much time to spend in the kitchen.

By preparing a few dishes ahead, and freezing them in single portions, you can avoid the daily chore of cooking. Soups are particularly economical, and easy to prepare in bulk and then freeze in single portions. If you have to provide packed lunches for your toddler, try freezing a few easily transportable dishes such as filo sacks (page 18) or Cheese and Rice Rissoles (page 22). They are tasty, nutritious and make a change from sandwiches. It is a good idea to have a few recipes up your sleeve for 'almost instant' meals such as Tuna Hash (page 22), Sardine Pâté (page 14) or Spanish Omelette (page 20). And for some fun recipes to tempt fussy eaters, why not try fish-shaped fish cakes or rice sandcastles?

Bean and Bacon Boats

Preparation time: 15 minutes + 50 minutes baking.
Freezing: not recommended. Serves 1 adult + 1–2 children.

This is a fun way to serve jacket potatoes. For a tasty alternative, melt a small knob of butter in a frying pan, sauté half a chopped onion until soft, add 125 g (4 oz) chopped cooked cabbage and cook over a low heat for 2–3 minutes until hot. Add to the mashed potato and continue as shown.

2 baking potatoes
2 rashers streaky bacon
205 g (7 oz) canned barbecue beans or baked

beans in tomato sauce
a small knob of butter or margarine
1 cheese single, cut in 4 triangles

❶ Preheat the oven to Gas Mark 6/200°C/400°F.

❷ Prick the potatoes with a fork, place them on a baking sheet in the oven and bake for 30 minutes.

❸ Place the bacon rashers on the baking sheet. Pour the beans into a small ovenproof dish, cover and bake alongside the bacon and potato for another 15 minutes.

❹ When the potatoes are tender, cut them in half, scoop out the flesh and mash with a little butter or margarine. Snip the bacon into small pieces and beat into the potato.

❺ Spoon the beans into the bottom of each potato shell and fill with the mashed potato.

❻ Return to the oven and cook for 5–10 minutes more.

❼ Place the potatoes on serving plates and push the cheese triangles into the potatoes to make sails. Serve immediately.

Lentil and Tomato Soup

Preparation time: 10 minutes + 20–25 minutes cooking.
Freezing: recommended. Makes 1.2 litres (2 pints).

There is very little preparation needed for this filling soup, which can be made in minutes from a few storecupboard stand-bys.

1 tablespoon olive or sunflower oil
1 onion, chopped finely
1 garlic clove, crushed
125 g (4 oz) red lentils

900 ml (1½ pints) vegetable stock
500 g (1 lb) carton creamed tomatoes
a few fresh basil leaves (optional)
bread sticks, to serve

❶ Heat the oil in a large saucepan and stir in the onion and garlic. Fry gently for 2–3 minutes until the onion is beginning to soften.

❷ Rinse the lentils and add them to the pan along with the vegetable stock.

❸ Bring to a boil and simmer for 15 minutes.

❹ Stir in the creamed tomatoes and simmer for 5–10 minutes more, or until the lentils are soft and mushy.

❺ Remove from the heat and add the basil leaves (if using). Allow to cool slightly then purée in a food processor.

❻ Return to the stove and reheat gently if required. Serve with bread sticks.

Sardine Pâté

Preparation time: 10 minutes.
Freezing: not recommended. Serves 6–8.

Sardines are a good source of nutrients. This tasty spread is an ideal way of serving them as it's quick to make and very versatile. Use as a sandwich filling, spread it on toast, or add extra yogurt and serve it as a dip with sticks of raw vegetables for a healthy snack.

125 g (4 oz) canned skinless and boneless
  sardines in olive oil
125 g (4 oz) full-fat soft cheese

a little lemon juice
3 tablespoons natural yogurt

❶ Drain the oil from the fish and discard. Mash the fish with a fork.

❷ Beat the cheese until softened slightly, then stir in the fish, lemon juice and yogurt. If preparing for very small toddlers, this is best done in a food processor where a smoother texture can be achieved.

Starry Pumpkin Soup

Preparation time: 20 minutes + 20 minutes cooking.
Freezing: recommended. Makes 1.2 litres (2 pints).

The star-shaped croûtons served with this soup make it a fun and attractive dish for toddlers. Use butternut squash if pumpkin is not available.

2 slices of bread
sunflower oil for frying
½ teaspoon paprika
1 onion, chopped
2 garlic cloves, crushed

750 g (1½ lb) pumpkin or butternut squash, peeled and cubed
900 ml (1½ pints) chicken or vegetable stock
salt and pepper

❶ Using a biscuit cutter, stamp out star shapes from the two slices of bread. You could also make a few moon shapes if desired.

❷ Heat about 5 tablespoons of oil in a frying pan and stir in the paprika. Add the bread and fry, tossing frequently, until the bread is crisp and golden.

❸ Remove the croûtons from the oil and drain on kitchen paper. Set aside.

❹ Heat 3–4 tablespoons of oil in a large saucepan and gently fry the onion and garlic until softened. Add the pumpkin or squash and fry for a further 5 minutes.

❺ Add the stock and bring to a boil, reduce the heat, cover and simmer for 20 minutes.

❻ Allow to cool slightly and purée in a food processor.

❼ Reheat gently and season to taste. Serve in bowls or mugs, scattered with the star-shaped croûtons.

Sausage and Bean Filo Sacks

Preparation time: 25 minutes + 15 minutes baking.
Freezing: recommended. Makes 16.

A variation on the ever-popular bangers and beans, these make an ideal addition to any lunch box.

250 g (8 oz) potatoes, peeled and diced
50 g (2 oz) mozzarella cheese, chopped
1 or 2 chipolatas or vegetarian sausages,
    cooked and sliced

220 g (7½ oz) canned beans in tomato sauce
270 g (9 oz) packet of filo pastry, thawed if
    frozen
sunflower oil for brushing

❶ Cook the diced potato in boiling water for 6–8 minutes or until just tender. Drain and set aside.
❷ Combine the cooked potato, cheese, sausage and beans together in a small bowl.
❸ Preheat the oven to Gas Mark 6/200°C/400°F. Lightly grease 2 baking sheets.
❹ Stack 3 sheets of filo pastry on top of one another, brushing oil between each layer. Brush the top layer with oil and cut

the pastry in 8 pieces about 10 cm (4 inches) square.
❺ Spoon a little of the bean mixture on to each pastry square and gather together the edges to make a bundle. Place on a baking sheet.
❻ Repeat with the remaining pastry and bean mixture. When all the sacks have been made, brush them with oil and bake for 10–15 minutes or until golden. Serve warm or cold.

Chicken and Banana Salad

Preparation time: 10 minutes.
Freezing: not recommended. Serves 1 adult + 1 child.

This flavour combination was a particular favourite of my son, who still adores bananas. It can be served as a salad on its own, and it also makes an ideal filling for pitta breads for older children.

125 g (4 oz) cooked chicken
1 banana
a little lemon juice
1 bunch watercress, washed and chopped

roughly
4 tablespoons Greek-style yogurt
pitta breads, to serve (optional)

❶ Cut the chicken in small bite-size pieces.
❷ Slice the banana and toss in a little lemon juice to prevent it from discolouring.

❸ Place the chicken, banana and chopped watercress in a bowl. Add the yogurt and toss until well coated. Serve in pitta breads if desired.

Spanish Omelette

Preparation and cooking time: 25 minutes.
Freezing: not recommended. Serves 2 adults + 2 children.

This tasty Spanish-style omelette can be eaten hot or cold. You could make it as a light meal to share with your child, or have it for your own supper and then add it to your child's lunch box the following day.

250 g (8 oz) potatoes, diced
4 tablespoons olive or sunflower oil
250 g (8 oz) frozen mixed vegetables, thawed
6 eggs

3 tablespoons milk
1 tablespoon snipped chives
a pinch of ground nutmeg
salt and pepper

❶ Cook the chopped potato in boiling water for 6–8 minutes or until just tender. Drain and set aside.

❷ Heat the oil in a heavy-based frying pan and gently fry the potatoes and mixed vegetables over a low heat for 3–4 minutes.

❸ Beat together the eggs, milk, chives, nutmeg and seasoning. Pour the mixture into the pan and stir until well combined with the vegetables.

❹ Cook over a low heat, pulling the mixture from the sides to the centre of the pan as it cooks. Tilt the pan so that the uncooked mixture runs to the edges.

❺ Continue to cook over a low heat until the egg mixture is just set and the underside is golden.

❻ Slide on to a plate and flip back into the pan to brown the other side. Alternatively, brown the top under a preheated grill.

❼ Serve hot or cold, cut in wedges, with crispbread and a salad if desired.

Cheese and Rice Rissoles

Preparation time: 15 minutes + 10 minutes chilling + 5–10 minutes cooking.
Freezing: recommended. Makes 8.

These tasty rissoles can be served hot or cold as a light meal or as part of a packed lunch. Serve with a salad or dip of your choice. Make sure that the nuts are chopped very finely if you are serving this to young toddlers.

125 g (4 oz) long-grain brown rice, cooked
50 g (2 oz) Cheddar cheese, grated
50 g (2 oz) full-fat soft cheese
50 g (2 oz) chopped cashew nuts

1 egg, beaten lightly
4–5 tablespoons oatmeal
4 tablespoons olive or sunflower oil

❶ Place the rice, cheeses and nuts in a mixing bowl and beat together until combined.
❷ Add enough egg to bind the mixture together. Divide the mixture in 8 and roll into rissole shapes.
❸ Roll each rissole in the oatmeal to coat. Chill for 10 minutes or until you're ready to cook them.
❹ Heat the oil in a frying pan and shallow-fry the rissoles until they are golden on all sides. Serve hot or cold.

Tuna Hash

Preparation and cooking time: 15 minutes.
Freezing: not recommended. Serves 1 adult + 1 child.

You can make this tasty and simple dish with a few ingredients that you probably already have to hand. It is a good dish for using up leftover potato.

1 tablespoon olive or sunflower oil
4 spring onions, sliced
1 celery stick, sliced
100 g (3½ oz) canned tuna in oil, drained

250 g (8 oz) cooked potato, mashed or cubed
¼ teaspoon dried mixed herbs
2 tablespoons tomato ketchup

❶ Heat the oil in a frying-pan and fry the spring onions and celery for 2–3 minutes or until softened.
❷ Add the tuna, breaking it up slightly with the back of a spoon.
❸ Stir in the potato, herbs and tomato ketchup. Toss over the heat until piping hot, taking care not to break up the tuna too much.
❹ Allow to cool slightly before serving. Serve on toast or with grilled tomatoes.

Fish Cakes

Preparation and cooking time: 20–25 minutes.
Freezing: recommended after step 4.
Makes 4 large or 8 small fish cakes.

Make small fish cakes for toddlers and larger ones for the rest of the family. For fun you can shape the mixture into fish shapes, either by hand or by using a biscuit cutter as a guide. Serve on a sea of peas, with carrots cut into smaller fish or starfish shapes. Try making a sun with a tomato half and mayonnaise sun-rays. You can use canned salmon or tuna for a more economical dish.

250 g (8 oz) salmon or cod fillet
500 g (1 lb) potatoes, cooked
1 tablespoon full-cream milk
a small knob of butter or margarine

1 tablespoon snipped chives
flour for dusting
sunflower oil for frying

❶ Steam or poach the fish for 5–10 minutes, or until the fish flakes easily. Leave until cool enough to handle.

❷ Remove the skin from the fish and double check for any stray bones. Flake the fish into a bowl.

❸ Mash the potatoes with the milk, butter and chives. Add to the fish and mix well.

❹ With floured hands, shape the mixture into rounds or fish shapes, and dust with a little more flour. Chill until ready to cook.

❺ Heat the oil in a frying-pan and shallow-fry for 5–10 minutes, turning once, until heated through and crisp outside.

Rice Sandcastles in a Meaty Sauce

Preparation time: 20 minutes + 30 minutes cooking.
Freezing: recommended. Serves 4 children.

Here's a truly versatile recipe with a fun way of serving rice. The meaty sauce is a simple bolognese sauce perfect for serving with pasta too.

175 g (6 oz) brown rice
450 ml (¾pint) water
1 tablespoon olive or sunflower oil
1 small onion, chopped finely
250 g (8 oz) lean minced beef or lamb
397 g (13 oz) canned chopped tomatoes with herbs

1 tablespoon tomato purée
1 tablespoon chopped fresh parsley
carrot flags, cut from thin slices of carrot and mounted on cocktail sticks (optional)

❶ Place the rice in a saucepan with the water and bring to a boil. Stir once, reduce the heat and simmer, covered, for 25 minutes, or until the rice is tender and the water has been absorbed.

❷ Meanwhile, heat the oil in another saucepan and fry the onion until soft. Stir in the mince and cook until browned, breaking it up as it cooks.

❸ Stir in the tomatoes and tomato purée. Simmer gently for 25 minutes.

❹ When the rice is cooked, stir in the parsley. Divide the rice between 4 lightly oiled dariole moulds if you have them, packing down well. If you do not have the moulds, use small cups or ramekin dishes instead.

❺ Allow the rice to stand in the moulds for 5 minutes, and then turn out on to individual serving plates. Top with a carrot flag if desired.

❻ Spoon the meat sauce around the 'sandcastles' and serve.

Note: *Take care that your toddler does not try to eat the flag cocktail stick. For young toddlers it is safer to remove the sticks before they tuck in.*

Family Meals

With ever-busy lives, most parents do not have the time to cook separate meals for their toddlers, and indeed this is not at all necessary. The recipes in this chapter have been devised with the family in mind, and most will serve 2 adults and 2 children.

Most of these recipes are also suitable for freezing, so if you need a regular supply of single main meals for your toddler, freeze these dishes in child-sized portions for use later on.

It is also a good idea to limit the salt intake of toddlers. As many of these recipes are flavoured with herbs and spices, you may find that you don't need to add any salt.

Chicken and fish feature strongly as they are easily digested and are ideal as the basis of first family meals. Mince is also ideal for toddlers because it is easy to chew. There is no need to include meat in every meal and you will find some tasty vegetarian ideas too.

Beany Cod Hot-Pot

Preparation time: 20 minutes + 40 minutes cooking time.
Freezing: recommended. Serves 2 adults + 2 children.

This is a filling family meal which makes a tasty change from the more traditional meat hot-pot.

500 g (1 lb) potatoes, peeled
2 tablespoons olive or sunflower oil
1 onion, chopped finely
400 g (13 oz) canned chopped tomatoes, drained with juice reserved
1 teaspoon cornflour
420 g (14 oz) canned cannellini beans, rinsed and drained
2 tablespoons fruity brown sauce
375 g (12 oz) cod fillet, skinned and cut in chunks
15 g (½ oz) butter or margarine

❶ Preheat the oven to Gas Mark 4/ 180°C/350°F.
❷ Parboil the potatoes for 5 minutes, drain and cool quickly under cold running water. Drain again and slice.
❸ Heat the oil and gently fry the onion until it just begins to soften. Mix a little of the juice from the canned tomatoes with the cornflour to form a smooth paste.
❹ Stir in the tomatoes with the rest of their juices, beans, brown sauce and cornflour mixture.
❺ Check the fish for any stray bones and add to the pan.
❻ Spoon half the fish mixture into a 1.2-litre (2-pint) deep ovenproof dish and arrange half of the potatoes on top.
❼ Repeat these two layers.
❽ Dot with the butter and bake for 40 minutes.

Savoury Fish Crumble

Preparation time: 25 minutes + 25 minutes baking.
Freezing: recommended. Serves 2 adults + 2 children.

Don't use crumble toppings for sweet dishes only. They are much quicker to prepare than pastry and make a tasty alternative to pies.

250 g (8 oz) white fish fillet (e.g. cod or
  haddock), skinned
250 g (8 oz) salmon fillet, skinned
450 ml (¾ pint) full-cream milk
250 g (8 oz) broccoli florets
25 g (1 oz) butter or margarine
1 small red pepper, de-seeded and chopped
25 g (1 oz) plain flour
125 g (4 oz) full-fat soft cheese

1 tablespoon chopped fresh parsley or ½
  tablespoon chopped fresh dill
salt and pepper
For the topping:
125 g (4 oz) plain flour, sieved
50 g (2 oz) sunflower margarine
50 g (2 oz) porridge oats
50 g (2 oz) Cheddar cheese, grated
30 g (1½ oz) packet salt and vinegar crisps
  (optional)

❶ Place the fish fillets in a pan with the milk and poach gently for 5–10 minutes, or until the fish begins to flake.

❷ Remove the fish from the milk and set them both aside.

❸ Meanwhile, blanch the broccoli florets in boiling water for 4–5 minutes or until just tender.

❹ Melt the butter in a large saucepan and gently fry the red pepper for 3 minutes until just tender. Stir in the flour and cook for 1 minute.

❺ Remove from the heat and gradually beat in the reserved milk. Return to the heat and cook gently, stirring, until slightly thickened.

❻ Stir in the cheese and parsley or dill and season lightly to taste.

❼ Add the fish, flaking it into chunks as you do so. Stir in the broccoli and spoon the mixture into a shallow ovenproof dish.

❽ Preheat the oven to Gas Mark 6/200°C/400°F.

❾ To make the crumble, place the flour in a mixing bowl and rub in the margarine until the mixture resembles fine breadcrumbs.

❿ Stir in the oats and Cheddar cheese. Lightly crush the crisps (if using) and add them to the crumble topping. Sprinkle over the fish mixture and bake for 20–25 minutes or until the top is golden brown.

Cheesy Chicken and Bacon Rolls

Preparation time: 15 minutes + 20 minutes cooking.
Freezing: not recommended. Serves 2 adults + 2 children.

Smoked bacon gives extra flavour to this delicious chicken dish, but you can use unsmoked if you prefer.

3 chicken breast fillets, skinned
6 rashers smoked streaky bacon, rind removed
a little wholegrain mustard

2 tablespoons olive or sunflower oil
150 ml (¼ pint) chicken stock
50 g (2 oz) Bel Paese cheese, cubed

❶ Place each chicken fillet between two sheets of clingfilm and beat with a rolling pin to flatten.

❷ Stretch the bacon with the back of a knife and slice each rasher in half lengthways.

❸ Spread a little mustard over the chicken breasts and lay 4 bacon pieces on top of each.

❹ Roll up the chicken breasts (with the bacon on the inside) and secure with a cocktail stick.

❺ Heat the oil in a heavy-based frying pan and brown the chicken rolls on all sides. Reduce the heat and cook the chicken for about 15 minutes until cooked through.

❻ Remove the chicken rolls from the pan and keep warm. Discard most of the fat, leaving any juices in the pan.

❼ Add the chicken stock, bring to a boil and boil rapidly for 1–2 minutes until slightly reduced.

❽ Reduce the heat and add the cheese, stirring constantly until the cheese melts.

❾ To serve, remove the cocktail sticks and slice the chicken rolls, allowing one complete roll for each adult and half a roll for each child. Serve with the creamy cheese sauce.

Special Chicken Curry

Preparation time: 20 minutes + 20 minutes cooking.
Freezing: recommended. Serves 2 adults + 2–3 children.

I first gave this to my son when he was about 1 year old – the mildly spicy, slightly sweet taste was an instant hit. Since then it has become a firm family favourite – not least because it is so easy to make.

4 tablespoons olive or sunflower oil

3 chicken breast fillets, cut in strips

1–2 mild Spanish onions, quartered and sliced

1–2 tablespoons mild curry paste

500 g (1 lb) carton creamed tomatoes

1 small cooking apple, peeled, cored and
    cubed

1 bay leaf

2 tablespoons mango chutney

150 ml (¼ pint) chicken stock

❶ Heat half the oil in a large saucepan and fry the chicken until browned on all sides. Remove from the pan and set aside.

❷ Add the remaining oil (if needed) and fry the onion until soft and beginning to brown. Stir in the curry paste and cook, stirring, for 1 minute.

❸ Return the chicken to the pan and stir in the tomatoes, apple, bay leaf, chutney and stock.

❹ Bring to a boil, reduce the heat and simmer, covered, for 20 minutes or until the chicken is cooked through.

❺ Remove the bay leaf and serve, cutting the chicken in smaller pieces if necessary. (This is easiest done with a pair of kitchen scissors.) This curry is delicious served with rice.

Creamy Chicken Bake

Preparation time: 20 minutes + 35 minutes baking.
Freezing: recommended (without topping).
Serves 2 adults + 2 children.

This is an ideal way of using leftover chicken. Occasionally, if time is short, I serve this dish without the topping, after simply heating it through on the hob.

50 g (2 oz) butter + extra for greasing
1 onion, sliced
½ red pepper, de-seeded and sliced
½ green pepper, de-seeded and sliced
75 g (3 oz) mushrooms, sliced
25 g (1 oz) plain flour
450 ml (¾ pint) full-cream milk
a pinch of ground nutmeg

50 g (2 oz) Bel Paese or full-fat soft cheese, grated
250–375 g (8–12 oz) cooked chicken, chopped
salt and pepper
For the topping:
30 g (1 oz) packet plain crisps or 30 g (1 oz) mildly flavoured corn chips
50 g (2 oz) wholemeal breadcrumbs
50 g (2 oz) mozzarella cheese, grated

❶ Preheat the oven to Gas Mark 4/180°C/350°F. Lightly grease a shallow ovenproof dish.

❷ Melt the butter and gently fry the onion and peppers until just soft. Add the mushrooms and fry for 3–4 minutes.

❸ Stir in the flour and cook for 1 minute, stirring.

❹ Remove from the heat and gradually' add the milk. Return to the heat and cook gently, stirring until slightly thickened.

❺ Season with salt, pepper and nutmeg and stir in the cheese. Cook until the cheese melts.

❻ Stir in the chicken and spoon the mixture into the prepared dish.

❼ Lightly crush the crisps or corn chips. Mix together with the breadcrumbs and cheese and sprinkle over the chicken. Bake for 30–35 minutes.

Home-Made Beef Burgers

Preparation time: 20 minutes + 20 minutes cooking.
Freezing: recommended. Serves 2 adults + 2 children.

I always make up a double quantity of these burgers and freeze them uncooked. If you do not make them too thick they can be cooked from frozen. Alternatively, defrost them overnight in the refrigerator. Beefburgers are only as good as the meat they are made from, so buy the best quality mince you can. Try making them with minced pork or lamb, and vary the herbs for tasty changes. You can make mini-burgers for very young children, as they are easier for small fingers to manage.

750 g (1½ lb) lean minced beef
1 small onion, chopped finely
50 g (2 oz) porridge oats
1 egg, beaten lightly
1 teaspoon chopped fresh mixed herbs or
 ½ teaspoon dried mixed herbs

a pinch of ground allspice
salt and pepper
To serve:
soft rolls or pitta breads
salad garnish
relish

❶ Mix together the minced beef, onion, oats, egg, herbs, allspice, salt and pepper until well combined.

❷ Divide the mixture into 6 large or 4 large plus 4 small balls. Push the mixture together well and then flatten slightly. Alternatively, you can use round biscuit cutters as moulds (there is no need to buy special burger presses). Place the cutter on a work surface and pack the required amount of meat into it, pressing down well. Slip the cutter off and repeat until all the mince is used.

❸ Shallow-fry or grill for 5–10 minutes each side, depending on the thickness. Serve in soft rolls or pittas, with a salad garnish and relish of your choice.

Sausage and Kidney Casserole

Preparation time: 15 minutes + 20 minutes cooking.
Freezing: recommended. Serves 2 adults + 2 children.

This is a tasty casserole and a good introduction to cooking and eating offal. This recipe makes good use of convenience products to produce a casserole in next to no time.

6 lamb's kidneys, skinned, cored and halved
6 chipolata sausages
1 small onion, sliced (optional)

175 g (6 oz) frozen mixed casserole
   vegetables
400 g (13 oz) canned chopped tomatoes with
   herbs

❶ Rinse the kidneys and pat them dry with kitchen paper. Set aside.
❷ Dry-fry the chipolatas in a heavy-based, deep-sided frying pan until browned on all sides. Remove from the pan and set aside.
❸ If necessary, add a little oil to the pan and fry the kidneys to seal, turning once. If using the onion, remove the kidneys from the pan, fry the onion until just softened, and return the kidneys to the pan.
❹ Cut the browned sausages in half and add them to the pan.
❺ Stir in the vegetables and tomatoes. Bring to a boil, reduce the heat and simmer for 15–20 minutes. Serve with a green vegetable of your choice.

Pasta with Tomato and Mushroom Sauce

Preparation time: 10 minutes + 10–15 minutes cooking.
Freezing: recommended. Serves 2 adults + 2 children.

This must be one of the easiest pasta sauces to make – it's quick, delicious and fresh tasting.

2 tablespoons olive or sunflower oil
1 small onion, chopped finely
1 clove of garlic, crushed (optional)
175 g (6 oz) mushrooms, sliced

500 g (1 lb) carton creamed tomatoes
a few fresh basil leaves, shredded
250 g (8 oz) pasta shapes of your choice
salt and pepper

❶ Heat the oil in a saucepan and gently fry the onion and garlic (if using), until they just begin to soften.
❷ Add the mushrooms and gently fry for 3–4 minutes more.
❸ Stir in the creamed tomatoes and basil leaves, bring to just below a boil and simmer gently for 10 minutes.
❹ Season to taste with salt and pepper if required.
❺ While the sauce is cooking, cook the pasta in plenty of boiling water for 10 minutes or as directed on the packet.
❻ When the pasta is cooked, drain well and serve with the tomato and mushroom sauce.

Casseroled Lamb with Leeks

Preparation time: 20 minutes + 30 minutes cooking.
Freezing: recommended. Serves 2 adults + 2 children.

This is a simple casserole which can be cooked on the hob. You can vary the vegetables according to what you have at hand. I have used leeks in this recipe as they have a milder flavour than onions, which some toddlers may prefer. You could add potatoes to turn this dish into a meal-in-one, but you may need to add a little extra stock.

375 g (12 oz) lamb fillet or lamb steaks,
    trimmed and cut in thin strips
2 tablespoons seasoned flour
3–4 tablespoons olive or sunflower oil

375 g (12 oz) leeks, washed, trimmed and
    sliced
375 g (12 oz) carrots, sliced
450 ml (¾ pint) lamb stock
1 tablespoon chopped fresh thyme

❶ Toss the lamb in the seasoned flour.

❷ Heat half the oil in a large saucepan and fry the leeks and carrots for about 5 minutes or until just beginning to soften. Remove with a slotted spoon and set aside.

❸ Add the remaining oil (if needed) and fry the lamb until sealed. Return the vegetables to the pan and add the stock and thyme.

❹ Bring to a boil, reduce the heat, cover and simmer for 30 minutes or until the lamb is tender.

❺ Serve with potatoes and a green vegetable of your choice.

Seaman's Supper

Preparation and cooking time: 25 minutes.
Freezing: recommended. Serves 2 adults + 2 children.

The fresh vegetables in this dish give it a delicious flavour. Although this will freeze perfectly well, its flavour is better when eaten fresh.

250 g (8 oz) tomatoes
250 g (8 oz) pasta shells
2 tablespoons olive or sunflower oil
1 small onion, chopped
2 courgettes, sliced
1 tablespoon cornflour

450 ml (¾ pint) tomato juice
a few basil leaves, shredded
350 g (12 oz) canned tuna in oil, drained
4 tablespoons wholemeal breadcrumbs
3 tablespoons grated Double Gloucester
    cheese

❶ Skin the tomatoes, if desired. To do this, make a small cross in the skins at the stalk end of the tomato and plunge first in boiling water for a few seconds and then in cold water. This will loosen the skins so that they can be easily pulled away.

❷ Cut the tomatoes into wedges and discard the seeds.

❸ Cook the pasta in plenty of boiling water for 12 minutes, or as directed on the packet.

❹ Meanwhile, heat the oil in a large saucepan and gently fry the onion until just beginning to soften. Add the courgettes and fry for 3–5 minutes, until just tender.

❺ Mix the cornflour with a little of the tomato juice. Add the remaining juice, the cornflour mixture, tomato wedges, basil leaves and tuna fish to the pan. Break the tuna into bite-sized chunks with the side of a spoon and allow the mixture to simmer gently for about 5 minutes.

❻ When the pasta is cooked, drain well and toss with the tomato and tuna sauce. Pour into a flameproof shallow dish.

❼ Mix together the breadcrumbs and cheese and sprinkle over the top of the pasta. Brown under a preheated grill and serve immediately.

Vegetable Chilli Pie

Preparation time: 25 minutes + 20 minutes baking.
Freezing: recommended (at end of step 6).
Serves 2 adults + 2 children.

Here is a tasty vegetarian version of shepherd's pie. You can make individual portions if you like – ramekin dishes are ideal for child-sized portions.

2 tablespoons olive or sunflower oil

1 large onion, chopped

1 garlic clove, crushed

2 carrots, sliced

2 courgettes, sliced

1–2 teaspoons mild chilli powder

400 g (13 oz) canned chopped tomatoes

2 tablespoons tomato purée

210 g (7½ oz) canned chick-peas, rinsed and drained

210 g (7½ oz) canned red kidney beans, rinsed and drained

500 g (1 lb) potatoes, peeled and chopped

2 tablespoons milk

1 tablespoon chopped fresh parsley

3 tablespoons grated cheese (optional)

❶ Preheat the oven to Gas Mark 5/190°C/375°F.

❷ Heat the oil in a large saucepan and gently fry the onion and garlic for 5 minutes. Add the carrots and courgettes and fry for 5 minutes more.

❸ Stir in the chilli powder, tomatoes, and tomato purée.

❹ Mash about half of the chick-peas with a fork. Add them to the pan with the remaining whole chick-peas and kidney beans and stir well. Cover and simmer for 10–15 minutes. (If the mixture becomes

very thick, add a few tablespoons of vegetable stock or a little tomato juice.)

❺ Meanwhile, cook the potatoes for 10 minutes or until soft. Drain and mash well with the milk and parsley.

❻ Spoon the bean mixture into a 1.5-litre (2½-pint) shallow ovenproof dish. Spread the mashed potato over the top and sprinkle with the cheese (if using) or brush with a little oil.

❼ Bake at the top of the oven for 20 minutes or until the top is crisp and golden.

all of a sudden he jumpe[d]
he shouted happily.
[ca]ll her 'Kitty.' "

Vegetable Risotto with Tofu

Preparation time: 20 minutes + 40 minutes cooking.
Freezing: not recommended. Serves 2 adults + 2 children.

Tofu is made from soya beans and is a valuable source of protein and calcium in vegetarian diets. Here it is added to a simple rice risotto to make a nutritious main meal.

250 g (8 oz) tofu (bean curd)

25 g (1 oz) butter

1 tablespoon olive or sunflower oil

1 small onion, chopped finely

4 baby corn, thickly sliced

1 small red pepper, de-seeded and chopped

1 courgette, diced

250 g (8 oz) mushrooms, quartered

250 g (8 oz) long-grain brown rice

600 ml (1 pint) vegetable stock

1 teaspoon yeast extract

1 teaspoon dried mixed herbs

❶ Gently squeeze out the excess moisture from the tofu in a clean kitchen towel. Cut in small cubes.

❷ Melt the butter and oil in a saucepan and fry the tofu gently for 3 minutes until browned. Remove from the pan and set aside.

❸ Add the onion and baby corn to the pan and cook gently for 3 minutes.

❹ Add the pepper, courgette and mushrooms and cook for 2 minutes more. Stir in the rice and toss over the heat for 1 minute.

❺ Return the tofu to the pan and add the stock, yeast extract and herbs.

❻ Bring to a boil, stir and reduce the heat. Simmer, covered, for 35–40 minutes or until the stock has been absorbed and the rice is tender.

❼ If you find that the rice is cooked before the stock has been absorbed, remove the lid and boil uncovered for a few minutes until the liquid has evaporated. Allow to cool slightly before serving.

Vegetable Cobbler

Preparation time: 20 minutes + 20 minutes baking.
Freezing: recommended. Serves 2 adults + 2 children.

Children love the tasty scones served with this vegetable casserole.

3 tablespoons olive or sunflower oil

250 g (8 oz) potatoes, peeled and cut in
   2.5 cm (1-inch) cubes

1 small parsnip, peeled and cut in 2.5 cm
   (1-inch) cubes

3 carrots, sliced

300 g (10 oz) leeks, washed, trimmed and
   sliced

250 g (8 oz) cauliflower florets

1 tablespoon cornflour

300 ml (½ pint) vegetable stock

150 ml (¼ pint) milk

½ teaspoon herbes de Provence

salt and pepper

For the cobbler:

175 g (6 oz) self-raising flour

1 teaspoon herbes de Provence

25 g (1 oz) butter or sunflower margarine

about 6 tablespoons milk

❶ Heat the oil in a large saucepan and fry the potatoes, parsnip and carrots for 5 minutes. Add the leeks and fry for 2 minutes more. Stir in the cauliflower.

❷ Mix the cornflour with a little of the stock. Add the stock, milk and cornflour mixture to the pan and heat gently, stirring, until the sauce thickens slightly.

❸ Stir in the herbs and a little seasoning and simmer gently while preparing the cobbler.

❹ Preheat the oven to Gas Mark 6/200°C/400°F. Sieve the flour into a bowl and stir in the herbs. Rub in the fat until the mixture resembles fine breadcrumbs.

❺ Add enough milk to form a soft dough. Roll out to about 2 cm (¾-inch) thick on a lightly floured work surface and cut in 4 cm (1½-inch) rounds.

❻ Spoon the vegetable mixture into a 1.5-litre (2½-pint) shallow, ovenproof dish and arrange the cobblers around the edge of the dish. Brush them with a little milk.

❼ Bake in the centre of the oven for 15–20 minutes or until the cobblers are golden.

Healthy Snacks and Treats

Toddlers need a high intake of calories relative to their size. As their stomachs are small, they often eat small meals, and so in order to consume the energy and nutrients they require, it is often necessary for them to eat little and often.

However, try not to let your youngster fill up on sweets, cakes and biscuits between meals. Instead, choose sweet and savoury snacks and treats that will not only help meet their energy requirements, but will supply valuable nutrients as well. Fresh fruit, dried fruit, sticks of fresh raw vegetables and bread all make ideal between-meal snacks.

Banana Malt Cake

Preparation time: 15 minutes + 30 minutes baking.
Freezing: recommended. Makes an 18 cm (7-inch) cake.

A moist and gooey cake which children adore, this needs very little sugar because of the natural sweetness of bananas.

2 ripe bananas
75 g (3 oz) soft sunflower margarine
175 g (6 oz) self-raising wholemeal flour
2 eggs, beaten lightly
2 tablespoons milk
50 g (2 oz) sultanas

32 g (1 oz) sachet instant malted chocolate drink
50 g (2 oz) light muscovado sugar
1 tablespoon demerara sugar
oil for greasing

❶ Preheat the oven to Gas Mark 4/180°C/350°F. Grease and line an 18 cm (7-inch) square shallow cake tin.

❷ Place the bananas in a large mixing bowl and mash them with a fork. Add all the remaining ingredients except the demerara sugar and beat with a wooden spoon or electric hand whisk until well combined.

❸ Pour the mixture in the prepared tin and level the top. Sprinkle with the demerara sugar.

❹ Bake in the centre of the oven for 25–30 minutes, or until springy to the touch and the cake just begins to pull away from the edges of the tin.

❺ Cook on a wire rack and serve cut in squares or fingers.

Cookies

Preparation time: 15 minutes + 15 minutes baking.
Freezing: recommended. Makes 24.

When I was developing this recipe, I tried many variations in the fat and sugar quantities and also in the proportion of wholemeal flour. This combination gave the best balance without sacrificing on the flavour or texture. So these home-made cookies not only taste delicious, but have less sugar and fat than most.

50 g (2 oz) sunflower margarine + extra for
  greasing
40 g (1½ oz) light muscovado sugar
1 egg, beaten lightly
3 tablespoons milk

75 g (3 oz) self-raising wholemeal flour
75 g (3 oz) self-raising flour
32 g (1 oz) sachet instant malted chocolate
  drink

❶ Preheat the oven to Gas Mark 5/190°C/375°F. Lightly grease 2 baking sheets.

❷ Beat together the margarine and sugar until light and fluffy.

❸ Gradually beat in the egg and stir in the milk.

❹ Stir in the flour and malted chocolate drink powder.

❺ Place rounded teaspoons of the mixture on to the baking sheets and flatten them slightly. Do not place too close together as the mixture will spread during cooking.

❻ Bake for 12–15 minute or until lightly golden. Allow to cool slightly on the baking sheets before transferring to a wire rack to cool completely.

Variations: For *Chocolate chip cookies*, add 50 g (2 oz) white or plain chocolate chips to the basic mixture.

For *Fruity cookies*, omit the malted chocolate drink and add an extra 25 g (1 oz) self-raising flour, a few drops of vanilla essence and 50 g (2 oz) sultanas, currants or mixed dried fruit.

Bread Pudding

Preparation time: 10 minutes + 5–10 minutes standing.
Cooking time: 40–45 minutes.
Freezing: recommended. Makes about 9 squares.

You do not need to use fresh bread for this recipe although stale bread will take longer to soak up the milk.

300 g (10 oz) bread (preferably wholemeal)
450 ml (¾ pint) full-cream milk
1 egg, beaten lightly
2 tablespoons sunflower oil
1 dessert apple, peeled, cored and chopped

125 g (4 oz) sultanas
1 tablespoon light muscovado sugar
1 tablespoon ground mixed spice
oil for greasing

❶ Preheat the oven to Gas Mark 4/180°C/350°F. Lightly grease an 18 or 20 cm (7- or 8-inch) square shallow cake tin.

❷ Cut the bread in cubes and place them in a bowl with the milk. Allow to stand for 5–10 minutes until the bread soaks up the milk, stirring occasionally.

❸ Beat the egg and oil into the bread mixture.

❹ Stir in the chopped apple, sultanas, sugar and spice until well combined.

❺ Spoon the mixture into the prepared tin and press down lightly.

❻ Bake in the centre of the oven for 40–45 minutes until golden on top. Allow to cool in the tin. Cut into squares and serve.

Fruity Flapjacks

Preparation time: 10 minutes + 30 minutes baking.
Freezing: recommended. Makes about 18.

You can vary the dried fruit in this flapjack recipe. I have used chopped peaches and dates, but you can try adding a combination of other dried fruits, such as sultanas, currants, raisins, chopped apricots, chopped figs or chopped cherries.

150 g (5 oz) butter or sunflower margarine + extra for greasing
50 g (2 oz) light muscovado sugar
2 tablespoons clear honey
75 g (3 oz) self-raising wholemeal flour

250 g (8 oz) porridge oats
50 g (2 oz) ready-to-eat dried peaches, chopped
25 g (1 oz) dried dates, chopped

❶ Preheat the oven to Gas Mark 3/170°C/325°F. Lightly grease an 18 × 30 cm (7 × 12-inch) shallow cake tin.

❷ Melt the butter or margarine, sugar and honey in a saucepan over a low heat.

❸ Remove from the heat and stir in the remaining ingredients, beating until well combined.

❹ Pour into the prepared tin and press down well. Bake in the centre of the oven for 30 minutes or until golden.

❺ Allow the mixture to cool slightly in the tin before cutting in squares. Transfer the squares to a rack to cool completely. Store in an airtight tin.

Chocolate/Carob and Orange Muffins

Preparation time: 10 minutes + 20–25 minutes baking.
Freezing: recommended. Makes about 8–9.

Look out for mini-muffin tins – they make fun, bite-size muffins which are ideal for the smallest of tots. They will take 15–20 minutes to cook.

125 g (4 oz) self-raising flour
125 g (4 oz) wholemeal self-raising flour
50 g (2 oz) light muscovado sugar
50 g (2 oz) plain chocolate or carob drops

grated zest and juice of 1 orange
2 eggs, beaten lightly
175 g (6 oz) thick set natural yogurt
oil for greasing

❶ Preheat the oven to Gas Mark 5/190°C/375°F. Grease the muffin tins well. (Do not use paper cases as this recipe contains no added fat and the mixture will stick to them.)

❷ Combine the flours in a large mixing bowl and stir in the sugar and chocolate or carob drops.

❸ Make a well in the centre and add the orange zest, juice, eggs and yogurt. Beat until all the ingredients are combined. Do not worry if the mixture looks lumpy.

❹ Spoon the mixture into the prepared tins, about three-quarters full.

❺ Bake in the centre of the oven for 20–25 minutes until well risen and golden. (If using mini-muffin tins bake for 15–20 minutes.)

❻ Transfer to a wire rack to cool slightly. These muffins are particularly delicious when served warm.

Cheesy Scones

Preparation time: 10 minutes + 20 minutes baking.
Freezing: recommended. Makes 12.

Savoury scones make an ideal between-meal snack. They can be served plain, spread lightly with butter, or served with a savoury spread. By making the scones in wedges, you cut down on preparation time and do not even need a rolling pin. However, if you do have time, why not make them more fun by cutting them into alphabet, animal or other shapes with biscuit cutters? You can let your little ones help with this task – a fun introduction to baking.

250 g (8 oz) self-raising flour
125 g (4 oz) self-raising wholemeal flour
75 g (3 oz) butter or sunflower margarine
3 spring onions, sliced (optional)

125 g (4 oz) cottage cheese
about 125 ml (4 fl oz) full-cream milk
50 g (2 oz) Cheddar cheese, grated
oil for greasing

❶ Preheat the oven to Gas Mark 6/200°C/400°F. Lightly grease a baking sheet.

❷ Place the flours into a mixing bowl and rub in the fat until the mixture resembles fine breadcrumbs.

❸ Stir in the spring onion (if using) and the cottage cheese. Add enough milk to mix to a soft dough.

❹ Turn the dough out on to a floured surface and lightly knead the dough into a ball. Flatten to make an 18 cm (7-inch) round, or cut in shapes using a biscuit cutter.

❺ Brush the top with a little milk and sprinkle with the grated cheese.

❻ Cut the round in 12 wedges and place the wedges on the prepared baking sheet. Bake the scones in the top of the oven for 20 minutes or until risen and golden.

❼ Cool on a wire rack before serving.

Easy Mini-Pizza Faces

Preparation and cooking time: 15 minutes.
Freezing: not recommended. Makes 4.

These 'cheat's' pizzas are easy to make and fun too.

Use the following suggestions for faces as a guide, and let your imagination make use of whatever you have in the fridge. Mushroom slices are good for ears as well as noses, and you can cut bits of pepper for noses and eyes as well as mouths. Spring onion slices can also be used for eyes, or shredded to make whiskers for animal faces.

2 soft wholemeal baps, halved
3 tablespoons pizza topping
50 g (2 oz) Cheddar cheese, grated
25 g (1 oz) Red Leicester cheese, grated

¼ red or green pepper, sliced in 4 strips
1 mushroom, sliced in 4
8 frozen peas
2.5 cm (1-inch) piece of courgette, sliced in 4

❶ Preheat the grill and lightly toast the bap halves on each side.

❷ Spread a little pizza topping over the cut side of each half. Sprinkle the Cheddar cheese over the baps, leaving a small space at the top of each.

❸ Sprinkle the Red Leicester cheese over the remaining space on the baps to make the 'hair'.

❹ Use the pepper slices to make mouths, a mushroom slice for each nose and peas for the eyes. Cut the courgette slices in half and use for the ears.

❺ Place the decorated baps under the grill and cook until the cheese melts.

❻ Allow to cool slightly before serving.

Dips and Sticks

Preparation time: 5–10 minutes per dip.
Freezing: not recommended.

Sticks of raw fresh vegetables, such as carrots, celery, cucumber or pepper, make ideal between-meal snacks as they contain a range of vitamins and when served with a dip they are very appealing to toddlers. You can easily make your own dips in a matter of minutes and always have one to hand in the refrigerator. Here are three simple ideas to choose from.

Hummus

438 g canned chick-peas, rinsed and drained

1 garlic clove, crushed

2 tablespoons sesame oil

2 tablespoons olive oil

2 tablespoons water

1 tablespoon lemon juice

1 teaspoon sesame seeds

a pinch of ground coriander

❶ Place the chick-peas in a food processor and purée.

❷ Add the remaining ingredients and process until smooth.

Peanut Butter Dip

175 g (6 oz) smooth peanut butter

½ teaspoon yeast extract

200 g (7 oz) Greek-style yogurt

½ teaspoon ground cumin

2 teaspoons lemon juice

❶ Place all of the ingredients in a bowl and beat together until well combined.

Tomato Cheese Dip

113 g (4 oz) carton cottage cheese
1 teaspoon tomato purée

2 spring onions, chopped
a pinch of paprika

❶ Place all of the ingredients in a bowl and beat together until well combined.

Sausage Whirligigs

Preparation time: 20 minutes + 20 minutes baking.
Freezing: recommended. Makes about 24.

A fun variation on the popular sausage roll, these whirligigs can be served at parties, as part of a light meal, or in a packed lunch. Use vegetarian sausagemeat if you prefer.

500 g (1 lb) pork sausagemeat
½ small onion, chopped finely
1 small dessert apple, peeled, cored and chopped

1 tablespoon chopped fresh sage
500 g (1 lb) puff pastry, thawed if frozen
1 egg, beaten lightly
oil for greasing

❶ Preheat the oven to Gas Mark 6/200°C/400°F. Lightly grease 2 baking sheets.

❷ Mix together the sausagemeat, onion, apple and sage until well combined.

❸ On a lightly floured surface, roll out half of the pastry to a rectangle about 25 × 30 cm (10 × 12 inches) and trim the edges.

❹ Spread half of the sausagemeat over the pastry, leaving a 1 cm (½-inch) border at one short end and a slightly wider border at the other.

❺ Brush a little beaten egg along the wider pastry border and roll up the pastry from the other end as you would a swiss roll.

❻ Cut the roll in 12 slices about 1 cm (½ inch) thick. Place the slices flat and spaced apart on one of the prepared baking sheets.

❼ Repeat with the remaining pastry and sausagemeat. Brush the tops of the slices with beaten egg and bake in the oven for about 20 minutes or until golden and puffy. Serve hot or cold.

Desserts and Drinks

The sensible approach when choosing a dessert is to have it include mostly fruit, eggs or milk rather than sugar. A piece of fruit can make a very pleasant end to a meal. Canned fruit in natural juice is also a good choice. Milk puddings are popular with many toddlers. Fruit mousses and fools are a good way of including fruit in the diet of those who turn their noses up at fresh fruit. Fruit crumbles are ideal too. When making desserts for toddlers, do not automatically add sugar just because you think the fruit is too tart. If you limit the sweetness of desserts from the beginning, you will probably find that your children will enjoy foods far less sweetened than you do.

Home-made drinks are another way of adding milk and fruit to your child's diet and are a healthy alternative to soft drinks.

Lemon or Orange Barley Water

Preparation time: 15 minutes + 25 minutes cooking + chilling. Freezing: recommended. Makes 750 ml (1¼ pints).

This old-fashioned drink is a great crowd pleaser at birthday parties.

2 lemons or 3 small oranges
65 g (2½ oz) pearl barley
900 ml (1½ pints) water

2–3 tablespoons clear honey
orange or lemon slices, to serve (optional)

❶ Pare the rind from one lemon or orange, taking care to avoid the white pith which will give the drink a bitter flavour.
❷ Squeeze the juice from the fruit.
❸ Place the barley in a sieve and rinse through with boiling water. Strain well.
❹ Place the barley in a small saucepan with the water. Add the lemon or orange rind. Bring gently to a boil and then reduce the heat and simmer gently for 25 minutes.
❺ Stir the fruit juice and honey into the pan, stirring until dissolved.
❻ Strain through muslin into a serving jug and chill thoroughly. Use within 24 hours. Serve with slices of orange or lemon floating in each glass.

Fruit Milk Smoothies

Preparation time: 5 minutes.
Freezing: not recommended. Serves 2.

Milk is a valuable part of a toddler's diet, providing calcium and important vitamins. If your toddler is a reluctant milk drinker, try serving this tasty shake.

1 large ripe banana or 125 g (4 oz) soft ripe
summer fruits (e.g. raspberries, strawberries
or blueberries)

vanilla ice cream (optional)
300 ml (½ pint) ice-cold full-cream milk

❶ Place the fruit and ice cream (if using) in a food processor or blender and briefly purée the fruit.
❷ Add the milk and blend for a few seconds more until smooth and slightly frothy.

❸ Pour into glasses and serve immediately. (A small scoop of ice cream can be added to each glass if desired.)
Variation: Add 150 g (5 oz) natural or Greek-style yogurt to the mixture to create a slightly tangy flavour.

Strawberry and Coconut Fizz

Preparation time: 5 minutes + 5 minutes cooking + chilling.
Freezing: not recommended. Serves 2.

This exotic-tasting drink is perfect for summer days.

125 g (4 oz) strawberries, sliced
2 tablespoons water
1 tablespoon block creamed coconut

1 tablespoon clear honey
sparking mineral water, to dilute

❶ Place the strawberries in a small saucepan with the water, coconut and honey. Cook over a low heat until the strawberries are mushy, breaking them up with the side of the spoon as they cook.

❷ Push the mixture through a sieve and chill.
❸ Dilute to the required consistency with sparking mineral water and serve immediately.

Apple and Apricot Crumble

Preparation time: 15 minutes + 35 minutes baking.
Freezing: recommended. Serves 3–4.

Dried apricots contain iron and make a delicious addition to a traditional apple crumble.

750 g (1½ lb) cooking apples, peeled, cored
   and sliced thickly
125 g (4 oz) no-soak dried apricots, halved or
   quartered
3 tablespoons orange juice

For the topping:
150 g (5 oz) plain flour, sieved
75 g (3 oz) sunflower margarine
50 g (2 oz) porridge oats
3 tablespoons light muscovado sugar

❶ Preheat the oven to Gas Mark 4/ 180°C/350°F.
❷ Place half the apple slices in a 1.5-litre (2½-pint) ovenproof dish and scatter the apricots over the top. Cover with the remaining apple slices.
❸ Pour the orange juice over the fruit.
❹ Place the flour in a mixing bowl and rub in the margarine until the mixture resembles fine breadcrumbs.
❺ Thoroughly stir in the oats and sugar.
❻ Pour the crumble mixture over the fruit and press down lightly.
❼ Bake for about 35 minutes or until the top is golden brown. Let cool slightly and serve with natural yogurt or custard.

Fruity Filo Stars

Preparation time: 20 minutes + 10 minutes cooking.
Freezing: not recommended. Makes 8.

Calcium is needed by toddlers for the development of strong bones and teeth, and yogurt can be a valuable source of calcium, especially for non-milk drinkers. Choose natural, whole milk yogurts and flavour them yourself.

4 sheets filo pastry
sunflower oil for brushing
1 ripe mango

150 g (5 oz) Greek-style yogurt
slices of kiwi fruit and strawberries, to
   decorate

❶ Preheat the oven to Gas Mark 6/200°C/400°F. Lightly grease a bun tray.
❷ Place a sheet of filo pastry on the work surface and brush with oil. Place another sheet on top and brush again with oil.
❸ Cut the sheets into 8 squares. Take 2 squares of filo and place one on top of the other at an angle. Place them in the prepared tin, scrunching the pastry slightly to form a star-shaped pastry case.
❹ Repeat with the remaining pastry and bake the cases blind for 5–10 minutes until just golden.
❺ Transfer to a wire rack to cool.
❻ Cut the mango flesh away from the stone. Remove the peel and purée in a food processor.
❼ Stir the mango purée into the yogurt and distribute evenly between the baked cases.
❽ Decorate with slices of kiwi fruit and strawberries.

Raspberry Mousse

Preparation time: 15 minutes + setting.
Freezing: not recommended. Serves 4.

Mousse is simple to make and popular with youngsters. For fun you could chill the mousse in small, shaped jelly moulds. You can make mousse with any fruit purée, and if you leave out the gelatine, you have a fruit fool.

250 g (8 oz) fresh or frozen raspberries,
   thawed
4 tablespoons orange juice
2 tablespoons honey

1 tablespoon gelatine
3 tablespoons water
200 g (7 oz) 8% fat fromage frais

❶ Place the raspberries, orange juice and honey in a liquidiser and process until puréed.

❷ Push through a sieve to remove the seeds and set aside.

❸ Sprinkle the gelatine over the water and dissolve over a pan of gently simmering water.

❹ Stir the gelatine and water into the raspberry purée. Fold in the fromage frais and spoon the mixture into glasses. Chill until set.

Topsy Turvy Banana Pudding

Preparation time: 20 minutes + 20 minutes cooking.
Freezing: not recommended. Serves 4.

A delicious coconut flavoured cake is cooked on top of bananas and then turned out in this topsy turvy pudding.

For the topping:
25 g (1 oz) butter
4 teaspoons light muscovado sugar
a little ground cinnamon
1 banana
For the cake:
50 g (2 oz) self-raising flour

50 g (2 oz) light muscovado sugar
50 g (2 oz) butter or sunflower margarine
25 g (1 oz) block creamed coconut, softened
25 g (1 oz) desiccated coconut
2 tablespoons milk
1 egg

❶ Preheat the oven to Gas Mark 4/180°C/350°F.

❷ Melt the butter and divide it between 4 ramekin dishes. Tilt the dishes so that the butter coats the sides thoroughly.

❸ Sprinkle a teaspoon of the sugar into the bottom of each dish, along with a little cinnamon.

❹ Slice the banana and divide between the dishes.

❺ Place all of the ingredients for the cake in a mixing bowl and beat until well combined.

❻ Divide the cake mixture between the dishes and bake in the centre of the oven for 20 minutes or until the cakes are springy to the touch.

❼ Allow to cool in the dishes for at least 5 minutes before turning out to serve.

Semolina with Spicy Apple and Pear Sauce

**Preparation time: 15 minutes + 15 minutes cooking.
Freezing: recommended. Serves 4.**

Milk puddings are ideal for including calcium in the diets of reluctant milk drinkers, but many take a long while to cook. Semolina, however, can be cooked in minutes. In this recipe it is served with a delicious apple and pear sauce, but if you are short of time, simply serve the semolina with fresh fruit or a little jam.

For the apple and pear sauce:
1 small cooking apple, peeled, cored and
   sliced
a small knob of butter or margarine
1 tablespoon honey
1 teaspoon ground mixed spice

8 tablespoons orange juice
1 pear, peeled, cored and chopped coarsely
For the semolina pudding:
6 tablespoons semolina
600 ml (1 pint) full-cream milk
1 tablespoon clear honey

❶ Place the apple slices, butter, honey, mixed spice and 2 tablespoons of the orange juice in a small saucepan and cook until the apple softens and becomes pulpy, breaking the apple up with the side of a spoon as it cooks.

❷ Add the chopped pear and remaining orange juice and cook for 2–3 minutes or until the pear is just softened.

❸ Meanwhile, place the semolina in a saucepan, add the milk and bring gently to a boil, stirring constantly.

❹ Reduce the heat and simmer for 5 minutes. Stir in the honey.

❺ Serve the semolina hot or cold, with the sauce either served separately or stirred into the pudding.

Index